I GREW UP WITH ELVIS
True but Little-Known Stories About the King—By Those Who Knew Him Best

CONTENTS

1	"What It's Like to Date Elvis" by Armand Archerd	3
2	"My Memories of Elvis—From Dates to Draft" by Cliff Gleaves	11
3	"The Day Elvis Made Me Cry" by Anita Wood	25
4	"I Laughed at Elvis..." by Jack McGuire (As told to Paul Neimark)	31
5	"I Grew Up with Elvis" by Nancy Anderson	40

Original publication dates:

"What It's Like to Date Elvis"
Movieland magazine, August 1957

"My Memories of Elvis—From Dates to Draft"
Movieland and TV Time magazine, September 1958

"The Day Elvis Made Me Cry"
Movieland and TV Time magazine, August 1959

"I Laughed at Elvis..."
Movieland and TV Time magazine, October 1959

"I Grew Up with Elvis"
Movieland and TV Time magazine, January 1960

Copyright © 1957, 1958, 1959, 1960 by Hillman Periodicals
ISBN: 978-1533027597

A. J. Cornell Publications

1 "WHAT IT'S LIKE TO DATE ELVIS"
by Armand Archerd

How would you feel if the phone awakened you at midnight—and it was Elvis, Elvis Presley, of course, calling to wish you a sweet and tender good night? How would you feel, too, if the very next morning you went to visit him, and found you couldn't get past the barriers which his position has erected to keep him apart from you—not you, really, but from everyone?

Maybe you'd be understanding. Maybe you wouldn't. It wasn't easy for Yvonne Lime to quite understand it. Yet, in a way, she knew it was inevitable. Friday night they had been out together until almost 4 a.m. and Saturday they were on the phone half the day. Sunday it was the same. Sunday night, he called to tell her good night. And then, Monday, he was back at work and once again it was: Elvis Presley, movie star; Yvonne Lime, girl from Glendale. Sounds like a corny soap opera, doesn't it? Sure, but life can be cornier—more tearful, more wonderful than any of the soap operas.

Elvis had in this friendship, perhaps, gone as far down the road to the altar as he had ever gone. Now the hour of decision was at hand.

Yvonne spoke hesitantly as she recalled her passage from the quiet, regular life of a girl from Glendale into Elvis's world. She had been trying to make her way in films as a competent actress—not a glamour girl, or cheesecake queen, but as an intense actress—not quite an ingénue, but not quite mature enough for adult roles.

Suddenly, because of Elvis, she found herself swept into a glamour world she didn't quite understand. She didn't want to be swept up by it—and she found that Elvis didn't want it either. Maybe this helped sweep them closer together—even while his world also seemed to try to keep them apart.

After visiting him at his home in Memphis, it all seemed beautiful, wonderful, hopeful. Then on her return, he was back on the phone to her. And the dating was hot and heavy.

It is Yvonne's laugh, her honesty, her apartness from the sophisticated world, that brought Elvis close to her on the set of *Loving You*. It was this trueness of Yvonne's that gave him the courage to ask her to leave Hollywood at the conclusion of the film and visit him and his folks, houseguest with them in

Memphis during the Easter holidays.

She had never before left home on her own, despite the fact that she was over 21. And she had never been out of California! She asked her mother if it would be all right. Her mother never had one fear for a moment, she said confidently.

The visit was to last four days, but after four days, he wanted her to remain. She wanted to stay, too. Her mom approved it on the long-distance phone.

It was real fun in Memphis. Yvonne was having a wonderful time. And so was Elvis. She really didn't know him before leaving Hollywood. But she knew him now. She also knew, perhaps, that it would end when the visit ended and possibly because it was best for both of them. But until that decisive hour, she was happy to stay longer.

"It's nothing serious," she said when she returned. That, perhaps, was what she was trying to convince herself, because she knew that, with his career, there could be nothing "serious."

"We discussed what would happen with his fans if he were married," she said. "I don't think they'd like it very much."

We agreed that this was the understatement of the week!

Even his fans, his friends in Memphis didn't like it, she pointed out, when he was dating her around town.

"We had to go out of town to get away from the crowd.

"We'd go hunting every day. Elvis, his cousins, Junior and Arthur. We shot at most everything, not really hitting anything at all. Just running, laughing, yelling. It was fun. P.S. I was the only girl in the group."

Elvis had gone home to escape, to take a deep breath, to relax. Yvonne was part of the feeling of being "at home."

"We stayed at his old home," she continued. "He wasn't going to move into the new one until it was completely redone. But even in this one he had six cars. We drove a different one each time we went out. What laughs! Yes, we even drove around town one day on the motorcycle.

"When we went into town, it was unbelievable. Everyplace we went, it was crowds, mobs. But they all loved him and he loves them, too. He still has his old friends from school. And we'd always stop and play pool with them. Elvis insisted."

Yvonne was slowly beginning to find out just how popular this fella she met on a movie set actually was! Even when he went to get his hair trimmed, there was always the mob of friends and fans, always watching, waiting, looking, grabbing.

Finally, they had to escape for a breather, and ran off to the lake, to sit on the bank, just to catch their breath, not utter a sound, hold hands and enjoy the aloneness and quiet, for a change.

Yvonne got a better chance to understand Elvis than perhaps any other girl. He took ill, yet he had promised the high school he'd attend their Saturday night dance and party. He could hardly get into his clothes that evening, he was so sick. But he got ready and Yvonne helped him into and out of the car, through the crowd, when she knew the pain was almost too much. Finally, after staying there several hours, she knew something had to be done, so she drove him to the hospital, where she stood by him while he was treated. The next morning, they went to church together. They were thankful.

"Please stay a few more days," he asked, and squeezed her hand.

"I'd like to; let me call California and ask my mother."

Yvonne had been getting up much earlier than Elvis during the visit. She'd go downstairs to the kitchen where his mom, also an early riser, was busy. Yvonne joined in the fixings and the two girls talked—about their favorite fella, Elvis. It was nice, Yvonne thought, and she could feel that Mrs. Presley liked it, and her, too.

When she called home, her mom said it was all right for her to stay a few more days.

The days whisked by and all too soon it was time for her to go.

"It was just awful," she admitted. "I didn't really want to go and Elvis wasn't happy about it, either."

And then, as if it were written into the script, Nature's forces entered the second act. A huge storm came up—thunder, lightning and all the special sound and light effects to make the moment more dramatic. The airport authorities weren't certain whether or not the planes would be taking off. Elvis and she huddled out on the ramp and wondered. The rain kept coming down, but the weather had cleared enough for the takeoff, the announcement said. Elvis came on the plane with her.

"And he stayed there until the very last minute, when he had to get off," she recalled. It was a long, long flight home to Hollywood.

He called to find if she'd gotten home all right. After that, there was the long wait for his return. Would the "Out of sight, out of mind" motto hold? It seemed so, when she didn't hear from him during the first few days of his arrival. He called, finally, explained how busy he was, that he had to run and would she please call him back later that day.

She tried to call back—but the operators in the hotel wouldn't put her through. They had orders not to put anyone through who wasn't authorized. She wasn't one of those on the list!

Elvis read in one of the columns that she had dated Jimmy Best, and he immediately got on the phone and called to ask about that. She laughed and told him: "What's this I read about you dating Debbie Smith?"

He laughed, and asked, "When are we going to get together?"

"How about the end of this week? Let's have a picnic," she said. "I'll bring my friends from Glendale;

you bring your boys from Memphis."

Great!

The caravan convened Friday evening. There were 44 kids, all set to go to the beach. Part of Yvonne's group went ahead to the assigned spot to set up the food. The rest followed an hour later. They arrived at the beach and—just like the script, again, a freak storm came up—almost a cloudburst.

Everyone ran for the cars, with Elvis shouting: "Keep driving north; we'll escape the storm." (It appeared to Elvis, apparently, that the storm was heading south.) They drove for an hour, an hour of hysterical laughs, but they didn't drive out of the storm—they drove *into* it.

Finally, at Trancas beach, they stopped and Elvis said, "Let's go back to the hotel. We'll have the picnic in my suite."

So, they all headed back—but one car didn't get the message. This was the car with the food!

Elvis got back. The cars with his buddies returned. Yvonne arrived. But when she, in her pedal pushers, tried to get past the lobby, and into the elevator to the floor of Elvis's suite, she was stopped.

"They thought I was someone trying to crash his place," she laughed. "I told them what had happened, but you can imagine how silly that sounded. Then I asked them to let me call him to prove it And they wouldn't allow any calls to him because they had their orders. 'OK,' I said, 'I'll just go down to the corner and call him from there and then you'll see.' What I didn't realize was that I'd still have to go through their switchboard! But it worked; they called and Elvis laughed himself sick, and said it was OK, of course."

The gang was starved—and no food. So Elvis sent out for hamburgers, baked beans, etc. It was more fun than they could ever have cooked up on the beach. Sure, it was a lot more hectic, too.

Then, someone suggested that Elvis sing. Fine—where's the guitar? There wasn't one in the suite; he had left 'em all at the studio! Let's go buy one, he said. Where? It was now almost 9 p.m. Someone remembered Music City on Vine Street.

They all piled back into the cars and caravanned down to the store. You can imagine the clerk's surprise when she looked up and there was Elvis Presley staring at her and saying: "I'd like to buy a guitar!"

The musical instruments department was closed! They returned to the hotel suite, where they laughed it up, singing and fooling around until it was practically three in the morning.

Elvis awoke late, called her first thing. Called her often. Called her to wish her good night, thereby making the weekend complete for Yvonne. It was wonderful—the time spent with Elvis—though on the morrow it might well be the beginning of a cherished memory for her and for Elvis. And maybe in her secret heart, Yvonne knew this was best and, possibly, what she really wanted.

2 "MY MEMORIES OF ELVIS—FROM DATES TO DRAFT"
by Cliff Gleaves

[Editor's Note: Cliff Gleaves, a native of Jackson, Tenn., near Memphis, met Elvis Presley in July of 1956 while working as a radio announcer for a Memphis radio station. Their friendship immediately grew, and later that year Elvis invited Cliff to go to New York with him, where Elvis was to make his first appearance on the *Ed Sullivan Show*.

This invitation opened the gates to a relationship that is known to all who are close to the two young men. Cliff, a Korean veteran, traveled with Elvis for almost two years until Elvis was drafted into the Army. He and Elvis were together constantly—and Cliff shared Elvis's ups and downs, his great triumphs and secret disappointments.

The two traveled over much of the world together,

and Cliff did his best to try to give Elvis a normal friendship in the sometimes-frantic world of the spotlight. Except for Elvis's family, Cliff knows Elvis better than any other person. They appeared together in three pictures—*Loving You, Jailhouse Rock,* and *King Creole.*

This story was written shortly after Elvis entered the Army. . . .]

It's hard to think back on two years and recall all the things that happened when Elvis and I were together. There were just too many of them, and the pace was sometimes so fast that now they are all jumbled together. But I imagine first you'd like to hear about his dating habits.

As almost everyone knows, Elvis doesn't "go steady" with any one girl. He likes to date different girls and do different things. Generally, he would rather be formally introduced to a girl before asking her out. It's not that he's shy—he's just not forward.

Where he goes on a date usually depends on the personality of the girl, and even then he might do the unexpected. He might be set on doing one thing, then change his mind while on the way, if he thinks his date might prefer to do something else. As for the stories printed about Elvis falling into a simplicity pattern with his dating, they're not true.

He's done everything on a date from dinner and dancing at Hollywood's Moulin Rouge Club to slipping into a pair of slacks and crash helmet and going on a midnight motorcycle ride.

Of course, Elvis doesn't drink or smoke. He's not the type of person that would, having been raised in a religious atmosphere. And naturally, no alcoholic beverages are served when he's on a date. Once he told me, "I don't see why people drink. It's their business, I guess, but to me there's no future in it."

When I first got to know him, Elvis was dating Barbara Hearn a lot in Memphis. They had known each other before he became famous, and their relationship didn't change after his popularity skyrocketed. They would go to movies (he's an avid movie fan), an occasional private party at someone's home ... and many times Elvis would pick her up and they'd go over to his house to listen to records or watch movies on the home projector that he owns.

One night, there were so many fans at his gate, Elvis couldn't get out of the house. He had a date with Barbara, and for a moment was stuck as to what to do.

Finally, he called her. "I hate to ask you this, honey, but I can't get out of the house. Would you mind if your mother brought you over here?" he asked. Barbara didn't mind, and Mrs. Hearn drove her over to the Presleys'. We all had dinner together that night—Elvis and Barbara, Mr. and Mrs. Presley, and I. After dinner, we went into the den and played pool on his small pool table. Elvis won—he's a whiz at pool.

Later we watched movies of the Indianapolis

"500" automobile race until about ten o'clock. By that time, the fans had thinned out outside, so Barbara, Elvis and I got into his Lincoln and went for a drive around town. We didn't go anywhere special . . . just rode around until 11:30, when Elvis took Barbara home. He likes quiet dates like that when he's in Memphis. It helps him to relax, and gets his mind off the million things that he carries around inside of him.

I'll never forget the first thing Elvis ever did that really impressed me. It wasn't at a performance or in a movie, or anything like that . . . it was how he reacted to an unknown fan's true wish. It really showed me how much Elvis's fans mean to him.

We were in New York in October of 1956 for the *Ed Sullivan Show*. It was snowing that night, and everything had been held up—as a result, we were behind schedule as we started into the entrance of the CBS studios. Network officials were with us, urging us to hurry, and there was a big crowd at the doorway pushing and shoving, blocking our way. As we tried to get through the crush of people, a small elderly lady somehow worked her way to the front of the crowd and called his name. Elvis stopped and turned to her.

She held out one of his albums. "Please, Elvis, would you sign this for me?" she asked.

One of the studio heads tried to get Elvis to keep moving, saying, "Come on, you don't have time for autographs now—50 million people are waiting to see you." But Elvis didn't pay attention to him.

He signed the lady's album cover, and then turned to the official.

"Listen," he said, "if she can take the time to buy my album, I can take the time to sign it."

Then we were through the doors and on our way to his television appearance.

Elvis loves nightlife, and when we were in Las Vegas for a two-week vacation last year, I guess we visited every club and every hotel in the city. Elvis had most of his dates there with Kathy Gabriel, Kitty Dolan and Sandy Preston (a New York model he met while he was there.) In Las Vegas he could show a girl the kind of time he really wanted to, whereas in other cities the fans made it hard for him to move around. Although there was some of the usual excitement of his presence in Las Vegas, he could circulate more freely—and freely he did!

One particular night he picked up Sandy about eight, and we went for dinner at the Sahara Hotel. I remember Edgar Bergen and the Mary Kaye Trio were featured on the floorshow, and Elvis was very impressed with Bergen's showmanship. Sandy and Elvis talked about show business, dating and the current interests they had together.

After dinner, we headed out to the Desert Inn, where Johnnie Ray was singing. We all went backstage, met Johnnie, and the two stars were mutually impressed with each other. Elvis thinks Johnnie is one of the most talented singers in show business, and that night he got the chance to tell him.

After leaving the Desert Inn, we looked in on the lounge of the Riviera Hotel, where they had continuous music. Elvis has a wide appreciation of all types of music, especially singers. If he likes a singer's voice, it doesn't matter what type of music he's singing—Elvis can appreciate it.

About 2:30 in the morning we went back to the Sahara, where Louis Prima and Keely Smith were giving a performance. Elvis was introduced to them, and right away the three became fast friends. (Whenever we would go back, Keely would dedicate a song to him, and Elvis got to know them quite well.)

We left the Sahara about 5 a.m. and drove around Las Vegas in Elvis's rented Cadillac for a couple of hours until a motorcycle shop opened. Elvis rented a motorcycle, bought leather jackets for Sandy and himself, and they went for a spin while I went back to the hotel. Elvis finally came in about 11 that morning, worn out but happy, and said to me, "Man, that was really a night."

Elvis is very partial to children. I guess being an only child himself has something to do with it, but he's just crazy about them. I'll never forget what he did for a group of them one night in 1956 when he was on a personal appearance tour.

We were in Shreveport, La., for a one-night show. About an hour before showtime somebody told him there was a group of youngsters afflicted with paralysis waiting to see him at the auditorium. Elvis usually doesn't get to a place of performance until just before he's scheduled to go on, to avoid being caught in the crowds and being late for his show. But this night, he left an hour early.

The children were lying on cots in a room off the stage, and Elvis pushed his way past the crowd in the main part of the building to get in to them. He spent more than an hour in the little room, chatting with the children and signing autographs for them. I could see that he was terribly moved, but he did a good job of keeping his emotions to himself.

Finally, after the show had been held up for nearly half an hour, the crowd was making a lot of noise and a policeman came in to escort him backstage. Somehow, the word got out to the audience why he was late, and when he came onstage, they didn't wait for him to sing a note. They just stood—all 11,000 of them—and cheered for what seemed like five minutes.

Elvis told me later that night, "Cliff, that ovation meant more to me than any single one I've ever had."

I think Elvis truly realized the full extent of his popularity in October of last year, when we went to Honolulu for public appearances. He didn't exactly know how he would be accepted in Hawaii. After all, it is pretty far from the mainland. During the boat trip over, he was nervous as to what the reactions of the Hawaiian people would be to his performances.

He got a big lift when he saw over 3,000 fans waiting for him at the dock—shouting and calling his name. They were orderly, but there wasn't any doubt that he was every bit as big a personality in Honolulu as he was on the mainland. But he got his biggest surprise when we got to our suite at the Hawaiian Village.

The management had delivered about 2,000 letters from his fans all over Hawaii. They were piled two or three feet high on one big table in the center of the room. Elvis looked at those letters for a long time—then walked out on the patio by himself.

After a few minutes, I followed him. He was standing at the end of the patio, his head down. I said, "What's wrong, Elvis? What's the matter?"

He looked up, the tears shining in his eyes. "I can't explain it to you, Cliff," he said. "All those letters! All those people way over here like me that much. It makes me feel so small."

This is just an opinion, but I think Elvis outdid himself in his shows over there, to please the Hawaiian people. I never saw him so affected that way over fan mail. He was tremendously impressed with their appreciation for him.

Elvis has had more than a few dates with big stars, but when he dated Rita Moreno in Hollywood, it was more than just two big-name people going out. They *really* had fun together.

Rita came on the set while we were making *Loving You,* and Elvis was introduced to her. Later that day he said to me, "She's cute, Cliff, don't you think? I'd like to date her." A day or so later, he called Rita and asked her to go out with him the next night. I could tell he was happy that she accepted. I was dating Laurie Wald, a Hollywood girl, so we decided to double for the evening.

Elvis called at Rita's apartment that night in his Cadillac limousine, wearing a black suit, white tie and black shoes. Rita met him in a black dress cut low in the back, wearing the white orchid Elvis had sent her in her hair. We went by for Laurie, and then over to the Moulin Rouge for dinner and to hear Dean Martin, who was headlining the bill there.

Rita and Elvis got to know each other right away. I think the big thing that brought them together was that they are both very fond of Spanish music, and a group of Spanish musicians were playing there that night. They chatted all through dinner—talking about acting, the movie business, and the city of Hollywood, which Elvis loves.

Elvis had asked some friends to drop into his suite at the Beverly Wilshire, so we went back there after dinner. About 30 guests came by, including Nick Adams—one of Elvis's closest Hollywood friends—Johnny Saxon, Rafael Campos, and their dates. We listened to the hi-fi, and talked.

Sammy Davis, Jr., put in a quick appearance later. He was forced into an impromptu performance on the spot. Elvis got a big bang out of Sammy's impersonations, and later Nick and I teamed with Sammy to give the group a laugh. It wasn't any serious acting or anything—just cutting up for a good time. Rita certainly did enjoy herself, and Elvis did, too.

About two o'clock in the morning, everyone suddenly realized they were hungry, So Elvis sent out for pizza for the whole party. A pizza-feast followed, and at 3:30 the gathering began to break up. I took Laurie home first, then Elvis dropped Rita off. He visited her several times after that, and took her to a movie once.

When Elvis got his draft notice, he wasn't too "shook up" about it. He had taken his preliminary physical examination nearly a year before his "greetings" arrived, and he knew it was just a matter of time until he was called. Naturally, nobody knew just exactly when he would have to go into the Army, and for that reason, Paramount had gone ahead with preliminary arrangements toward the filming of *King Creole.*

Elvis's original induction date was to be January 15 [1958]. He wanted to go ahead and be taken in then, and not put it off. But he knew Paramount had spent a great deal of money and advance preparation on *King Creole,* and if he was drafted without being able to complete the film, the studio would lose everything it had invested in the picture. Even then, he hesitated to ask for a deferment.

However, knowing it was the best thing to do, Elvis did write his draft board a letter just before Christmas, asking for a three-months extension to finish the picture. Paramount also wrote. The deferment was immediately granted.

Elvis's biggest worry about going into the Army was that he wouldn't be treated like any other boy called to serve his country. After he received his draft notice he told me, "Cliff, I'm just another guy. I couldn't stand it if I got any special treatment when I go in. Millions of other fellows have taken this step, and I'm no better than anyone else."

He told me he didn't care what he did in the service, but whatever job the Army placed him in, he was going to try and do his best.

So Elvis spent most of the last three months of his civilian life away from home making *King Creole*. It was shot in Hollywood and Louisiana, and after it was completed in March, he came home to spend his last ten days of civilian life with his parents and friends.

He dated Anita Wood pretty regularly during his last few days at home. We would stay at his house until late nearly every night, then Elvis would drive over and pick up Anita and a whole group of us would go out to one of the city's roller rinks. Elvis rented it after it normally closed for the night, and we skated until almost dawn several nights. I'm sure his impending induction was on his thoughts, but he managed to have a lot of fun with the people he liked the best.

The weekend before he was drafted, Elvis bought Anita a 1956 Ford for a going-away present. It wasn't a flashy gift, but one that came from sincerity, and it gave Elvis a lot of pleasure to give it to her.

The night before he was scheduled to report for

induction, he and Anita went out on a quiet movie date. He took her home about midnight, then went back to his house and spent the rest of the night talking with friends.

He got to bed about 4:30, and Mr. Presley called him about 5:30, so he had only an hour's sleep. How he got through that day as tired as he was I'll never know—but you'd have thought he had slept 12 hours.

I met Elvis at the entrance to his home about 6:30 and followed him in another car while he drove with his parents to the draft board. He thought it might be the last time he would be able to see them alone for several months.

The reporters and photographers immediately recognized his car when he pulled up in front of the draft board, and rushed him as soon as it had stopped. He got out, greeted them with a cheery "Good morning, gentlemen," and said, "This is a pretty big day—if you think I'm nervous, you're right!" But he didn't show it at all during the draft procedures. He was pleasant and genial with everyone, posing for pictures with his parents and other draftees.

After the roll was called, Elvis and the other men were taken to the examining station by Army bus. There they got their last physical examinations, filled out papers, and finally took the oath of Army allegiance.

The time at the examining station was bad on Elvis, but he took it with good nature. The Army had made arrangements for full coverage of his induction, and as a consequence Elvis didn't have a minute of his own as did the other draftees. Whenever a break came in the business of processing, he was constantly asked to make statements, pose for pictures, and make tape-recorded interviews.

His parents were allowed to come in and sit in the station lounge. [Elvis's friend] Judy Spreckels had flown in from Hollywood and was with them. Whenever he could, Elvis came over to sit with them and talk. After lunch, there wasn't much to do until he was sworn in, so he took a nap on a couch in front of the TV set. It was amazing that he could sleep amid all that noise, but when he woke up, he didn't look as tired as he did earlier in the day.

Elvis had heard that he and the rest of the men were to be sent by bus to nearby Ft. Chaffee, Ark., right after they were sworn in. So he asked a sergeant, "Would it be all right if my girlfriend came out to say goodbye?" The sergeant gave his permission, and Elvis had someone call her. In a few minutes Anita drove up in her new present. When she came into the lounge, she and Elvis held hands briefly, then sat down to talk.

The swearing-in ceremony was very impressive. As each man's name was called, he would take a step forward, and after all had done this, they raised their right hands and repeated the oath of allegiance. Elvis was the second man to have his name called. He repeated the oath in a strong, clear voice, and it was obvious that he was proud.

Army officials chose Elvis to lead the group of new soldiers during their trip to Ft. Chaffee. This meant Elvis was to take care of all papers, see that time schedules were kept, and take general charge of the group. He accepted this—his first Army responsibility—without comment.

When the bus arrived, everybody went outside so that Elvis could spend a few seconds saying goodbye to his folks. When he came out, he went up to the group where Anita was standing. She was trying hard not to cry, but the tears just couldn't be held back. They looked at each other for a moment.

Then Elvis put his arms around her, pressed his cheek next to hers, and murmured, "Goodbye, baby."

"Goodbye, Elvis," Anita said tearfully.

Then he picked up his suitcase, boarded the bus, and started out for two years of Army service.

It's quite a change, this move from the country's top star to Private, U.S. Army. But I know Elvis will make it easily. We've been through a lot together, and I've seen him in all kinds of situations. I have never seen him when he wasn't completely aware of the situation around him—and he does the right thing instinctively.

For the next two years, Elvis will be doing a job for his country. I know he'll do his best.

3 "THE DAY ELVIS MADE ME CRY"
by Anita Wood

I'll never forget the day Elvis made me cry.

But first, let me go back a bit. . . .

I know that most of you who are reading my words would give your summer vacation just to walk into a movie house on the arm of Elvis Presley, or dance cheek-to-cheek with him at a big formal in his honor.

Before I dated Elvis, I felt the same way. I would have given anything—I mean *anything*—to be out with the one and only Elvis Presley, and have the whole world know about it.

That was before I really did go out with Elvis, before I became his "number one girl" as he put it, and before I grew to know him not just as a celebrity and secret sweetheart of millions of girls like myself, but as the tenderest and gentlest boy I had ever met. And the most mature, too.

But I can honestly tell you that I truly wish Elvis were a truck driver, or a mailman or a farmer—just so long as I could be with him and not have a dozen reporters and hundreds of people always staring and following our every move.

I told this to a close girl friend once, but she laughed and said that if Elvis was an ordinary truck driver, I'd miss all the excitement and commotion that goes on every time we walk into a theater or place to eat. She didn't understand, I'm afraid. With fans and newspapermen continually swarming around him, what chance does any one person have to really get to know Elvis?

I remember the time that he said I was his *number one girl,* and gave me the beautiful cocktail ring that I'm wearing right now. If any of a million other boys across the country had said that about the girl they were going with, that would have been that. But not with Elvis. Right away some reporter printed his statement, and the next day letters were pouring in from all over the United States asking who I was and telling me that I certainly wasn't good enough for Elvis and so on. I was on the verge of tears almost every moment for the next few days.

Perhaps *you* resented me too, at the time. But I honestly hope not. Just put yourself in my place. How would you feel if you received insulting letters from strangers just because Elvis liked you?

Elvis had to issue a public statement saying that we

were "just good friends" and we couldn't see each other for the next few weeks. I took that time to answer every letter I'd gotten, telling the girl that I knew Elvis was something special and that I didn't feel I was good enough for him yet, either. And during each of those days—and even at this very moment—I said to myself: Oh, if only he were a truck driver, none of this would happen! If only we could hold hands in the balcony of a theatre without having a thousand pairs of eyes looking at us instead of at the picture!

Now, I don't want any of you to think that I'm sorry Elvis is so very talented and hardworking. I think he has fantastic abilities, and I respect him for it. The movies he's made, particularly *King Creole*, show that he has immense acting ability. And his records, the ballads and religious songs as well as the rock 'n' roll, prove how versatile and well-endowed a singer he is. But it's what Elvis is as a *person* that's most important to me.

If someone says that he doesn't like the way Elvis sings or acts, that's one thing. But if I ever hear anyone say he doesn't like Elvis *as a person* when he hasn't even met him, then I'm ready to take that person on. I know that may not be ladylike, but I don't care.

Until I met Elvis, I hadn't gone steadily with one boy for longer than a few dates. It wasn't that I wanted to play the field, it was just that I couldn't seem to find anyone who had all the qualities I wanted in a person.

Then Elvis came along.

In the beginning, he impressed me because he was so famous and talented, and because he bought me so many extravagant presents—like a car! But soon I began to see the person behind all this, and I realized that Elvis Presley was the tenderest, most sensitive person I had ever known.

When he wasn't signing an autograph or talking to some reporter, we'd get to talk, and the more he talked, the more I saw what a genuine, real human being he was. Sometimes he'd be so serious and mature, speaking about all his goals in life, like being a great actor. And sometimes he'd act so gentle and whimsical that you'd want to pet him like you would a playful kitten.

Let me tell you now the story that I haven't told anyone else, and I think you'll know what I mean.

After he'd given me the car and so many other expensive gifts and jewelry, I said to him one night, "Elvis, you're too extravagant with me. Don't get me any more gifts, much as I appreciate them. Just sitting in a show with you or sipping a soda is enough for me." He laughed and said he was going to go right on being extravagant, though. So finally I told him that if he was going to keep buying me things, there was one present I wanted more than I could say: a little dog. It was something I'd wanted for a long time and never had—a nice, cuddly puppy. After that, whenever he'd give me a gift I'd mention the puppy, sometimes very quietly or in an offhand manner, but once in a while I'd come right out and say it.

He just kept brushing it off, though, and changing the subject. If I'd bring it up again, he'd say something like, "Aww, who wants an ole dog?" I kind of thought it was funny, since Elvis loves animals and children so much. I've known him to come late to an appointment or a date because he stopped off to help a stray he saw in the street. But, finally, he left for the Army with nice goodbyes and a mention that he'd call me every week (he doesn't like to write), but without ever saying one word about the dog.

I tried not to let it bother me too much. I figured that he was awfully busy, what with his career and getting ready for the Army. So when he called me long-distance from Europe once or twice a week, even though we'd talk for as long as 45 minutes sometimes, I'd never bring up the dog. I was waiting for him to mention it, but he never did.

On Christmas Eve, 1958, I was sitting at home with my parents, and I'll admit my thoughts were with Elvis in Germany, when suddenly the doorbell rang and I heard a man say, "Special delivery for Anita Wood!" I ran to the door and there was the most adorable little toy French Poodle I'd ever seen! It was all white with a big red ribbon around its neck, and on the ribbon was a card that said "Merry Christmas, Anita—Elvis."

Well, all I can say is that I can never remember being as surprised or as happy.

I sat right down and bawled like a baby.

To think that all those times when I'd mentioned

the dog to Elvis and he shrugged it off like it wasn't important, he was actually planning to get me one. He was just waiting until the moment when it would mean the very most to me—Christmas Eve—when we'd be three thousand miles apart.

I named the puppy "Littlebit," but he means more than a *little bit* to me.

That's just one example of the *real* Elvis. It has nothing to do with the fact that he's a famous singer and a wonderful actor. He'd be Elvis whether he was a doctor, lawyer or Indian chief. Except that if he were one of those, then people would have a better chance to know him for the rare and wonderful person he is.

4 "I LAUGHED AT ELVIS UNTIL . . ."
by Jack McGuire (As told to Paul Neimark)

I'm what you might call a "hardboiled" public relations man. I've been in this business a dozen years now, I've met most of the big names in movies and TV, and I've been pretty disappointed with more than a few. Too many times I've seen how fast some stars can turn off their smiles, and also how fast the lack of a good director or echo chamber can turn off their talent. So, naturally, I smiled cynically when some of Elvis Presley's friends told me that he was "really a great singer." And I laughed out loud when they said he was "a genuinely nice guy."

I was handling publicity and arrangements for Elvis's first big concert in Chicago. The sold-out show was scheduled for 8:00 p.m., and since Presley had to leave town for another engagement the same night, a major press conference was scheduled for 6:30. I was sitting with about 200 reporters and interviewers in a club near the concert stadium, when suddenly a boy came up to me with a telegram. *Dear Jack McGuire,* it read. *Plane connections slow from last appearance. Elvis will be one hour late for press conference. Col. Tom Parker.*

I called for silence and read the telegram to the people gathered in the club. After I finished, an aggravated stir began to circulate through the room. Mutterings of "Who does he think he is?" and "I'll bet he did it on purpose, the prima donna," and "He probably thinks he's too good for us," reached my ears. I tried to be objective because the fact was that Presley couldn't help his tardiness at all, but I'll have to admit that underneath I felt much the same way as the others. I'd seen a lot of young stars let quick fame and fortune go to their heads, and I figured Elvis wasn't any exception.

Everyone was pretty disgusted when he finally rushed into the club at twenty minutes to eight. It was what we call a real bad scene, and yet no one had walked out, because they all wanted to see just what this young man really was like. They were reporters. Their job was to find the truth.

The minute Presley walked into the room, something changed. I saw it in the faces of the reporters, and even noticed it in my own attitude. This young singer was warm, and human, and a gentleman. And it wasn't put on—we'd all been in this business long enough to spot a fake. When he said, "Glad to meet you," he *meant* that he was *glad to meet you.* Gradually, the group began warming up to Elvis. They could sense that he was the genuine article—a tremendously successful star who had still retained his humility.

A little girl had snuck in with her hound dog; she wanted Elvis to pose with it. One of the doormen ran up and tried to take her out, but Presley intervened. "Hey, hey, Mister," he said. "Of course I'll pose with this little lady's doggie." Then, with all kinds of powerful men and women of the press waiting to talk to him, Elvis took time out to pose for a picture with the child's dog. He petted it and asked her what its name was, but he also gave the doorman an affectionate punch on the arm so that there wouldn't be any hard feelings. A few minutes later, two disc jockeys from a radio station in Michigan elbowed their way through to Elvis. They wanted to tape an interview with him and take it back to Detroit.

"We don't have time," one of Presley's personal press agents insisted. "It's only a half hour till he goes on, and this press conference was strictly for Chicago, anyway. Right, McGuire?"

I didn't know quite what to say, but before I even had a chance to answer, Elvis broke in. "Now, I can't disappoint these nice fellows when they came all the way from Detroit to see me, Al," he said. "By all means they can tape an interview with me, though they may have to hold it to five or ten minutes." The two deejays were overwhelmed! Never had a star, especially one of such great magnitude, gone that much out of his way for them.

To make a long story short, in just 50 minutes Elvis had each and every member of our crowd in the very palm of his hand. Including yours truly. As I walked with him from the club to the back of the theater (a measure we had to take if he wasn't to be stopped for hours by fans and thus delay his concert), I thought to myself: "Well, this kid may not be much of a singer, but he sure is a nice guy."

Twenty minutes later, after the applause and screams had died down and the standing audience was once more in their seats, I began to change my mind about Elvis's singing, too. He was much more of an artist than I'd thought; in fact, he was a perfectionist at his music. I realized that the occasional snatches of his records I'd heard on the radio while driving to my office, plus the comments of some of my "sophisticated" friends, had combined to prejudice me against his ability. Actually, when I listened to Elvis Presley in a complete concert, I discovered the versatility and natural richness in his voice for the first time, to say nothing of his fine stage presence. And I found Presley's gyrations—which I'd never seen but had laughed at the loudest—to be a fundamentally appropriate and highly dramatic extension of his art.

As the night went on, I took Elvis around town for a few hours to meet some more people. On the way from one place to another we talked, and more than ever I really got to know Elvis for the sincere, real guy he is. He talked about his career and how much better he wanted to be as an actor and singer, he talked about his family that he said was the best in the world, and he talked about his fans. In typically humble Elvis style, he confided to me that he thought his fans overestimated him, and he only hoped he could live up to their confidence in him.

My conversations with him came in bits, since we were on the move every minute from one place to another, talking to people and shaking their hands; but what he did say I remember, so strong was the impression it made on me.

"Do you mind if I call you *Elvis?*" I asked, as we sat down to order dinner.

"I'll never forgive you if you don't," he answered kiddingly.

I looked up at him. "I can see you're a little tired, and Colonel Parker told me that you hadn't had four hours' sleep in the last two days. Doesn't all this traveling get you? You don't have to do it, you know."

"Oh, it's kinda rough sometimes, Jack, I'll admit. Once in a while I stop and ask myself: What town am I in now? Crazy as that seems, it all goes so fast and you fly to so many places and meet so many people in just a few days that you really get them mixed up once in a while. But I want to do it. I think I owe it to my fans to see them in person and—"

The waitress had come up to take our order. She was a trim and attractive girl of about 19, and Elvis wasn't too tired to give her an approving glance, plus a big smile. "Eyes on the table, Presley!" I joked, after she'd taken the orders and left.

"You want me to act like an old man like you?" he kidded right back. "How old are You, Jack?"

"Thirty-four," I admitted.

"Thirty-four . . ." he said, far away in his thoughts.

"What'll you be doing when you're that ancient, Elvis?"

He thought for a minute, but you could see that he already knew the answer, that he had a well-formed plan in his mind of exactly where he was going for the next ten years. "Well, Jack," he answered, "for one thing, I'd like to be a really top-notch actor. I'd like to do parts which will have real depth."

"You know, I think I should tell you that I didn't like your singing before I heard you tonight. I figured you were just another young guy—"

He held up his hand and smiled that ear-to-ear smile again. "You don't have to say it. Whether you like me as a performer or not is only a matter of taste."

"But what about all these people who criticize you? The self-appointed judges of public taste who call you names and even think what you do is morally wrong?"

"I don't mind them. They have a right to their opinions. Of course, as far as the moral question goes, I can't see that. As a matter of fact, I kind of pride myself on having high morals."

The waitress brought the food and we dug in. As soon as Elvis put the fork to his mouth, however, a group of press people found us and gathered around.

I didn't really get to talk to him again until we were safely in a cab, whizzing off to another party.

"So tell me what you do for kicks, Elvis, when you aren't running from place to place singing or making movies," I asked.

"Oh, probably nothing different from anyone else—although, in a couple of months, I'm going to be getting a two-year vacation—the Army."

"I heard about that. I guess you'll have it made there, though, if you pull a couple of the right strings. . . ." I prodded him.

Suddenly, I saw his face harden. He wasn't mad, but you got the feeling that *something* was wrong. "What's the matter?" I asked. "I say the wrong thing?"

"No," he replied, "it's just that I don't believe in that."

"In what?"

"Pulling strings in the Army. I'm there to do a job for the country, same as any other guy. That may sound a little corny, but it's the way I feel, Jack."

"Now, don't get me wrong—I agree with you," I told him. "I did my service, too, and any guy that tries to chicken out gripes me. But you've done a lot of favors for a lot of people—heck, I've read you gave away about a dozen cars, and I saw the way you acted tonight with the reporters—so there's no reason you shouldn't get a break in return, is there?"

"Yes, there is. Whatever I did for anyone, I did 'cause I liked them. If the Army likes me, it can promote me, too. But I'm going to have to earn it first."

I didn't want to admit that I'd only been prodding him to see if he was really OK. What I'd said was what most guys would say, a kind of gripe about things in general just for the sake of small talk, the kind of talk you don't expect most people to take seriously. But I was beginning to realize that Elvis wasn't most people, and I respected him for speaking up.

The cab pulled up at the hotel, and I took out my wallet to pay the fare. Elvis pushed my arm aside and handed the driver a five-dollar bill. "Keep it," he said. The fare was only $3.15.

"Hey!" I said. "You can't do that. I've got an expense account that covers this."

"I know," he smiled. "So do I."

We made about four private parties and two more press gatherings in the next couple of hours, plus being mobbed several times by people on the street who recognized Elvis.

I said goodbye to Elvis at 2:30 a.m. at Midway Airport, where he was taking a plane to another concert. Rough schedule, I thought. I complained about getting up at eight in the morning, but probably the only sleep this man's gotten in the last week has been on planes, and yet he still makes an effort to be polite and understanding to everyone he meets.

I'd laughed at Elvis until that night, but as the plane took off and drew away to a single speck of light in the distance, I wasn't laughing anymore. Instead, I felt lucky—lucky that I'd had the privilege of getting to know such a good guy and such a big talent. And maybe I was a bit disappointed, too—disappointed that it was all over so soon.

The next morning, the reviews in the papers were fabulous. *"Presley talented—off stage he's calm, 'nice guy'"* ... *"Elvis hypnotizes fans—and this reporter"* ... *"Elvis Presley a gigantic success—should be on top for long time to come."*

But the item that rang the loudest bell for me wasn't on the front page or in big, black type, but way in the back of one paper. It was just a brief news report of all the hundreds of ushers and policemen and firemen needed for the concert, but one quote by the tough Captain assigned to protect Elvis caught my eye. "That is a nice boy," the Captain said. "A real sweet guy. In fact, I think he's one of the nicest people I've ever met."

Of course, by that time I didn't need anyone to convince me that Elvis Presley is a really *great* guy—in every single sense of the word.

5 "I GREW UP WITH ELVIS"
by Nancy Anderson

Young Bob Presley drummed his bare heels against the high porch side and looked at his cousin, Elvis, with wonderment. Bob was older than Elvis, almost three years older, and he felt responsible for the kid. He was a good enough boy, Elvis was . . . smart, too . . . but a dreamer, and Bob felt compelled to set him straight. It was time he faced a few facts of life.

"Now, Elvis, I'm telling you," said 13-year-old Bob, "you're wrong about Santa Claus. You can't go around believing in Santa Claus all your life. People will laugh at you!"

The pair were sitting on the edge of a neighbor's porch in East Tupelo, Miss., and for nearly an hour they'd been arguing about Santa Claus. Bob was persuasive . . . Elvis was unconvinced.

After Bob's final thrust, the younger boy didn't answer right away. His bare feet were swinging against the porch side, too, but they didn't hang down as far as Bob's. Thoughtfully, he chewed a blade of grass and studied a little eddy of dust blowing up at the edge of the narrow street.

Then he shook his head.

"You're wrong, Bob," Elvis said. "You just don't know what you're talking about. I know you're wrong, and I'm going home and ask my mother."

Slowly he slid down from the porch edge into the yard. He picked up a homemade wooden gun (the kind that shot rubber bands), whistled for his dog, and walked across the yard to his house.

"I'm sorry you're so mixed up, Bob," he called. "Goodbye. I'll see you later!"

Bob Presley, sitting now on his own porch across the street from where the Santa Claus discussion took place, grins as he recalls it.

"I don't know yet," he says, "what Elvis's mother told him when he went home to ask about what I'd said. Whatever it was, he'd believe her. He did whatever his mother said, believed whatever she said and that was one of the reasons he wouldn't believe *me*. His mother had told him there was a Santa Claus, and he knew she knew more than I did."

Bob isn't sure, either, why he wanted to disillusion his young cousin. Possibly, from the height of a three-year age advantage, he wanted to appear wise. Maybe he wanted to impress Elvis by cynicism. But if he did, it didn't work. Elvis wasn't shaken or impressed. He simply hung onto his ideals . . . the ideals implanted at home.

And, for that reason, the Santa Claus episode is typical of Elvis's boyhood. The effects of his upbringing weren't easily counteracted. They haven't been yet.

Bob and Elvis played together throughout grammar school until Elvis moved to Memphis. Elvis was born in a little house just up the street from the house in which his cousin lives, and later he moved to a house across the street from Bob. There were more than 90 children in a stretch of two or three blocks, so the boys had plenty of company.

"We played," said Bob, "about the same things all boys play. Elvis and I made guns to shoot rubber bands, played cowboys and Indians . . . stuff like that. But, and I mean this honestly, he's one boy who never got into any kind of trouble."

Bob rocked gently as he talked, and glanced at his parents for confirmation. His father, Noah Presley, is Elvis's great uncle. His mother is Elvis's Aunt Christine.

"I can tell you *why* he never got into any trouble," Aunt Christine broke in. "There's never been a boy in the world closer to his mother than Elvis, and he wouldn't have done anything under any circumstances to hurt her."

"Well, now," Bob countered, "he wasn't too quiet or shy or anything like that. Elvis is like his daddy in one respect. Both of them are always joking. But he didn't get into fights or talk back to his teachers or play hooky."

On the question of Elvis's conduct, teachers bear Bob out, but they differ with him as to Elvis's musical ambition. . . .

"I can't remember a thing about him singing," Bob says. "He never mentioned to me any interest in music so far as I recall. In fact, he never mentioned what he wanted to do when he grew up. Of course, he sang in church."

But Elvis's fifth grade teacher, Mrs. J. C. Grimes, and her husband vividly recall the well-behaved little boy's musical talent. Mr. Grimes operates a furniture store and remembers how Elvis's grandfather brought the child into the store to sing for him.

"We were all proud of Elvis's singing when he was a boy," Mr. Grimes beams. "He's been criticized by some, but everybody here in the neighborhood where he lived thinks the world of him. I guess he knows it, too, because he came back into the store not too long age after he'd made a big name for himself.

"I was busy with something, and I heard somebody asking for my wife. I looked up, and there stood Elvis. He was wearing a black shirt and pink trousers and had a pink Cadillac parked outside."

There's little wonder that Elvis asked for Mrs. Grimes, because she had a part in his first musical triumph.

"He used to sing in the class programs," she explains, "and could sing one song, 'Old Shep,' so beautifully the children would almost cry. Elvis didn't sing rock 'n' roll then or move around when he sang. He has a sweet voice and sang with such sincerity that every child in the room who'd ever had a dog was touched by 'Old Shep.'

"The Alabama-Mississippi fair was going on and featured a singing contest of some kind. I told the principal of our school that a little boy in my room sang so well he ought to be in the contest. The principal took him to the fair to compete, and Elvis won.

"I've read somewhere he took his own guitar to the contest, but he didn't. He had to borrow one when he got there. I remember."

Mrs. Grimes feels almost like a second mother to Elvis, she's known him so long. She knew him years before he was in her class at school.

"The first time I remember seeing him," she recollects, "I stopped by to speak to his grandmother, Mrs. Smith, who lived with Elvis's parents. Mrs. Presley had told me that Mrs. Smith had known my mother, and I wanted to talk with her about that.

"Anyway, I met Elvis that day. He was a nice, clean, polite little boy. He always was."

A fellow student recalls that in the seventh grade Elvis was much in demand for home room programs. Incidentally, the boy who arranged many of the home room programs is now in Germany in the Army, too. When he gets out, he plans to take a graduate degree in music.

East Tupelo, Miss., the town in which Elvis was born, is full of Presleys and their kin. And here, in addition to good manners and high ideals, Elvis developed a strong awareness of family bonds. This is a typically Southern trait.

"Naturally," Aunt Chris says, "You've read how crazy he was about his mother. When he was away from home working, he'd call her on the phone all the time.

" 'Hello, Baby. How are you?' he'd say. After he got bigger, he always called her Baby.

"When he was a little fellow living across the street from us, his mother kept close watch on him. Even if he came over here to play, she generally came with him. He was her only child, you know, and she'd lost his twin. She liked to keep an eye on him.

"Many a time we've sat right here and talked about how well our boys played together."

Mrs. Christine Presley surveyed her living room with the unpainted siding walls and the dining room beyond with fruit on the table. The house seemed to be full of boys of all ages.

One, a boy in his middle teens, leaped into the conversation.

"I didn't know Elvis when he lived here," he contributed, "because I'm from Texas. But I know he thinks a lot of his family, because I saw him at a hotel in Texas a while back. Fans and autograph hunters had surrounded him and were climbing all over him. I got through and told him who I was, and as soon as he found out I was his cousin, he got away from the rest of the people to talk with me about the folks at home."

Elvis created quite a stir on the quiet residential street in East Tupelo the last time he visited Cousin Bob, Aunt Christine and Uncle Noah....

East Tupelo is a small town, just three miles from Tupelo on the road toward Alabama. There's a single traffic light and a filling station where Elvis's Cousin Arnold works. If the eastbound traveler turns left at the light and follows the narrow blacktop around a curve, he's in the block where Elvis played as a boy and where his Aunt Chris and uncle Noah live today. More than likely, he'll see Aunt Chris sitting on the porch.

"I was sitting right here one day," she says, "when a big, cream-colored car pulled up in front. I thought it was a salesman and was trying to run into the house when somebody called me."

As Aunt Chris peered to identify the caller, the car door opened and a tall, familiar young man climbed out.

"Chris," he said, "I don't believe you know me!"

At the further sound of the voice, Aunt Christine gave a high cry of surprise and ran down the steps.

"Why, Elvis, honey," she laughed, "it's you! Come on up here and sit down. What in the world are you doing here?"

Elvis mounted the steps and threw an arm around his aunt.

"I can't stay long," he grinned, looking around the familiar yard. "I'm supposed to be in Atlanta in six hours, and I don't think I can make it now, but I *couldn't* go by without speaking."

A dog got up from the end of the porch where he'd been sleeping and came over to sniff the stranger.

"Hey, fellow," Elvis said, stroking the dog's ears, "what's your name?"

Aunt Chris said the dog was named Tippy, but before she could say anything else neighbors were streaming into the gate. The local hero was home, and he deserved a hero's welcome!

A friend from across the street was in such a rush to see Elvis he hadn't taken time to put on his shirt and shoes.

"I'm sorry to come over here this way," he apologized, "but I didn't want to miss you."

"Gosh," Elvis envied, "I wish I could get by without my shoes and shirt. I'd be a lot more comfortable!"

Everybody wanted to see Elvis, to see how he'd changed, to tell him how proud they were of him. It was a memorable afternoon on a usually quiet street.

People in East Tupelo know Elvis as well as they know each other. They know him better than most people do, because they've known him all his life.

But in East Tupelo, it's hard to get a story about him.

"I'll tell you why it is," says Cousin Bob. "We can't

tell you anything exciting about Elvis, because we knew him just as another boy. And besides, he was always a good boy. When a fellow's in trouble or doing bad things, you remember them. But the good things are forgotten. Elvis was always a nice boy . . . still is. About the only story you can get in East Tupelo is people think the world of Elvis.

"You can tell his fans that, I guess. The people who've known him always and who know him best can say only good of him."

And that's probably the heart of the story. Elvis Presley's greatest success isn't as a singer (a few people don't like to hear him sing) or as an actor (a few people don't go to his pictures) but as a human being. Because, in that respect, *everybody* likes him.

If you doubt it, just go ask questions in East Tupelo.

Made in United States
Troutdale, OR
08/10/2025